SOULFUL SERENADE: A POETIC VOYAGE

EXPLORING THE DEPTHS OF EMOTIONS THROUGH HEARTFELT VERSES

MARINA GOMES

To my hero - my dad, my best friend - my mom, my husband and to my friends.

Thank you for always supporting me and helping me to pursue my passion. This book is dedicated to all of you! Hope you enjoy reading them.

With all my love,

Marina Gomes

Contents

Contents

Contents

Foreword

In "Soulful Serenade," Marina Gomes beckons us into the ethereal domain of poetry with her lyrical compositions, each verse an intricate weaving touching the innermost core of the heart.

With a mastery on her language and a profound sensitivity to the human experience, Marina invites readers on a journey of introspection, where emotions are unveiled and truths are illuminated. Her poems resonate with the echoes of universal longing, joy, pain, and hope, offering solace and inspiration to weary spirits.

I met Marina during the lockdown in 2021. We crossed paths through our work groups and instantly bonded during a virtual corporate cultural event collaboration. Marina isn't just delightful but incredibly talented too. Her ability to connect quickly makes every interaction with her a delight.

As you turn the pages of this collection, allow yourself to be enveloped by the tender embrace of Marina's verses. Let her words wash over you like a gentle breeze, awakening dormant emotions and igniting the flames of imagination. For in "Soulful Serenade," Marina Gomes has crafted not just a book of poems, but a timeless symphony of the soul.

Here's wishing Marina and Soulful Serenade success, always!

~Sneha Acharekar

Sneha Acharekar is a writer by passion and profession. An active blogger and poetess on various online sites. She has five published books to her name, and has won the WriteFluence award for her short-stories collection 'Aboveground'. Her poetry and short stories have also been published in most international compilations curated by WriteFluence. Sneha is also the creator of 'Stories by Sneha', a podcast that plays on all podcasting channels.

Preface

Soulful Serenade is my debut poetry book. Poetry has always been a wonderful medium that allows the heart to express what we may otherwise hold back from sharing. From the tender whispers of love, to the echoes of loss, from the triumphs of happiness to the valleys of despair, each poem in this collection encapsulates the varied emotions that one goes through in love's journey.

I draw inspiration from nature and human relationships. There is a profound connection between the two and the closer we are to nature, the deeper our understanding is of the complex emotions we all experience. In "Soulful Serenade," you will find verses that unveil the experiences of love, loss, longing, despair, hope and resilience. I hope you find comfort and inspiration as you navigate your own journey.

I am deeply grateful to the people who inspired and supported me. To you, dear reader, thank you for embarking on this poetic journey with me. May these poems be a sanctuary for your soul, a reminder that you are not alone.

With deepest gratitude and love,

Marina Gomes

Acknowledgements

Sneha Acharekar for designing the beautiful book cover and for writing the foreword for my poetry book. You are a gifted writer, a wonderful person with a beautiful heart and a woman of many talents.

My fellow poets from Instagram who, time and again, posted lovely prompts online to help poets like me ignite the creative flame through dark nights. I want to call out their IG handles and would urge readers to check out their pages for a beautiful read.

In no particular order: IG handles - @portofpoetry, @if.pages.could.talk, @writefluence @blooming_positivity

Prologue

The book is divided into different themes. Feel free to explore the journey on your own by going straight to the theme that suits your state of mind, or sail with me from the beginning and live the experiences and make them your own.

No matter how you go through this journey, each turn will unravel something stirring; you may feel a sense of deja-vu or be filled with nostalgia as you relate the verses to your own emotions.

1. BUDDING

When exactly does one understand what being in love actually means?

For some, it may be during teens, when hormones are raging in our bodies and rationale defeats us. Whereas, some may go through entire adolescence glued to academic books and projects and even the mere thought of love may feel repulsive. And then there are some, who fall in love long after their friends are all married and have a family and they are just beginning to feel the mad exciting rush they never felt before. To all the people who have ever felt the tingling feeling, that rush of adrenaline, the butterflies in their stomach, the poems in this chapter will evoke that first love all over again.

ENCHANTED

I really can't explain what I feel

Every time I am with you.

Like a traveler who finds an offbeat road and

Enjoys the journey without knowing where it's going to lead;

Meeting you has been an enchanting journey,

And I am enjoying every moment of it.

When you speak to me, I hear palm trees rustling in the breeze.

When you hold my hand, I am drenched with sirimiri.

I steal a moment to look into your eyes,

And I'm instantly lost in a maze.

I really can't explain what I feel every time I am with you.

Am I me anymore?

Coz I've never felt this way before...

DISGUISE

And again today, he walked past her.

Every day she hoped she would see him just once,

And yet every time he passed by her,

She wished she could be invisible.

Her palpitating heart tried hard to slow down,

Her frenzied eyes stayed glued to the screen.

Her wandering mind paused

And focused on just one thing:

To not turn; no, not an inch,

Lest she face him.

Blood rushed to her face,

Her hands were cold,

Her throat choked,

All she wanted was for him to pass by.

And just when she thought it was over,

She heard the deep but gentle voice asking her,

"Hey! How are you?"

Like a chameleon that disguises

And changes colors and textures,

She replied with perfect poise,

"I'm having a great day! And you?"

And it ended with a smile and another great act!

THE TECTONIC AFFAIR

We met like two tectonic plates,

Rapidly moving towards each other.

The gravitating energy was too powerful.

Would we collide, or slide gently side by side?

Would we converge, or would we diverge?

Amidst the uncertainties and the unknowns,

The unanswered questions and the undesigned accidents,

The heart dances in turmoil.

Catastrophic waves sweep over me—

A tsunami of emotions is what I fight to stop.

The movement is subtle, yet rapid;

The fault lines develop...

A risky affair!

Seismic currents swell within me,

The undercurrents grow stronger,

The hot magma flows,

Violently shaking my core,

And finally, for now, it's all quiet.

The plates carry on their usual drift

Until they face each other again...

TORNADO

Good heavens!

The tornado struck without warning

And pulled everything into its vortex.

The red peony shrub was caught unawares.

Shaken she was, but she put on a brave face.

The whirlwind was too strong for her;

She leaned on the wall, lest she should fall.

She was determined to stay strong,

But she knew the pretense wouldn't last long.

She prayed the tornado would pass and let her breathe again.

It seemed like an eternity,

And yet she found the blather rather amusing.

At last, the storm passed by.

She watched as it glided gently over

To the other side of the universe,

Unaffected by the turmoil it created

In the red peony shrub's world...

ELEVEN STEPS

Don't ask me how I come up with these silly things

When I'm with you.

Like the other day, I counted the number of steps

We walked together.

11... yeah... 11 steps is all we walked,

From the aisle to the door.

And if counting steps was silly,

What would you say if I told you

I walked back and forth on the same steps

10 more times, and then as an afterthought,

I walked yet again, replaying the moment

Like a broken record on an old vinyl tape

Or like a scene that needs continuous re-takes.

I did that till I realized how silly it was,

And after a hearty laugh,

I came back to the superficial sanity

Of this world again.

PICTURE PERFECT

I can paint you with closed eyes,

Coz that's what I do every night.

I start outlining your face,

Your face—the heart-shaped one that defies time.

I trace your thick eyebrows,

Your brows—like rolling hills,

They slide gently over to the other.

I move on to your cheeks,

Your cheeks—I make gentle strokes with my fingers

On your chiseled cheeks.

I gasp as I entrap myself in your mesmerizing eyes,

Your eyes—a whirlpool of mystery is what they are!

Don't ask me how I escape them!

I run my finger around the curves of your lips

Your lips— an archer's bow is what they are,

Launching arrows in my heart.

And just when I think I'd stop,

You blow me away with your smile,

Your smile, that boyish, coy smile is enough

To bring the stars down from their celestial glory.

All I want to do is paint this picture each night

And wake up each morning

To find a reason to see you again.

HYPHENATED NAMES

No comma can separate us anymore,

The unspoken ellipsis

We fill in with our sweet nothings...

We slash the stars from the heavens

And drop them in our glass jars.

We orbit the Earth,

For tonight the Pink Moon will be ours.

We ignite the icy heart of Eris

With caramelized quotations of our "love's cadence."

Oh! Our amorous exclamations

Reverberate throughout the galaxy!

I write our hyphenated-names on your bare heart

And find comfort in your loving em{brace}

FOR NOW, THIS IS ENOUGH

Love may not last forever, but the time we spent

Making wonderful memories is eternal.

Love may not last forever,

But every time I remember today's day,

I will have a smile on my face.

We didn't make any promises of a lifetime, no, not one,

For we both know too well

That promises are empty deceptions.

But when you remembered what my favorite flowers are

And took the effort to bring me the blue flowers,

I felt loved.

When you sang the lines of the song I requested

At the karaoke bar, though you were mighty shy,

I felt loved.

When we impulsively decided to watch an open-air movie

And you altered your plans to join me,

I felt loved.

When you listened to all my stories without interrupting,

Although you are known to be quite a restless listener,

I felt loved.

When you spoke without inhibitions about yourself

And all the stories that no one has heard before,

I felt loved.

When you put your jacket on me coz the sea breeze was cold

And we were walking barefoot on the wet sand,

I felt loved.

When our fingers brushed accidentally against each other

For a split second, we both froze and looked into each other's eyes

And smiled, not knowing what to make of it,

I felt loved.

When it was time to bid goodbye, there was a long silence

As there was so much to say, so much to hear,

So much to feel, and yet we both knew it was time to leave,

So, we just sat next to each other,

And the noise of silence was drowned

By the thudding of our heartbeats,

I felt loved.

When you put your arms around me,

kissed my forehead gently and held me close to your heart,

I felt loved.

It is those little things you do, the kind words you say,

The gentle touches, the loving gazes—

I feel loved every time.

My heart has finally found solace

And a calm resting place.

I don't know if this will last forever, but,

For now, this is enough...

2. SENSUAL

Sensual love is a profound and intimate connection between two individuals characterized by a deep appreciation for each other's physical and emotional being, encompassing a strong desire to engage all senses, from the touch of their hand, to the taste of their kiss, the scent of their skin, the sound of their voice.

The poems in this chapter celebrate the beauty and pleasure of intimacy, igniting sparks of passion and creating moments of profound joy and fulfilment.

SURRENDERED SENSES

I love the sound of the two syllables

That make up your name,

Like the sound of Jal Tarang;

They are a melody to my ears.

I love the feel of your presence around me,

Like the mist that engulfs the garden at dawn;

Your presence is enough to make me bloom.

I love the sight of you in my thoughts,

Like the robin, I sing when I see you.

I love the taste of your salted wounds,

Like the forest ravaged by wildfire

That grows back rejuvenated; I heal too.

I love the fragrance of your woody notes,

Of pine, patchouli, and cedarwood.

You own me and my senses—heart, mind, and body.

I am captivated and enraptured by you,

Hopelessly and helplessly in love with you...

A SUMMER NIGHT

I lost the battle tonight; I was defeated by your thoughts.

They overpowered me, knocked me down, and left me breathless.

I am swept away by the tidal waves of passion.

I force myself out of my bed, stand by the window

And watch the antique moon idling away,

Staring at the haphazard constellations

That peep out of the blue and black sky.

Like a jester, they laugh aimlessly.

The indigo clouds cast a veil on the stars

Sprinkled across the heavens.

A selenophile that I am; I want to drink the moonlight tonight,

And dance to the cadence of its silvery shadows.

My pink babydoll swirls and flirts with my body.

I let the summer breeze hum a soulful serenade,

And kiss my cheeks tenderly.

How I wish it was you instead!

How I wish this night would never end!

CRANBERRY JUICE

Let's ditch coffee today,

Let's savor some cranberry juice.

You can taste it off my lips if you choose.

The scarlet sip slithers off the corners of my lips,

And snakes its way down to my neck, and further down.

Savor the taste and its ruby-red richness;

The texture of summer's exuberance in a single drop.

Let's spill it on our bodies, let it wash over us

And create a cranberry moment where we feast on each other.

Let us merge in a crimson embrace,

And dissolve in this sweet indulgence.

HUNGRY

I'm hungry for your love,

Like a sunflower yearns for sunlight.

The ecstatic moments we enjoy

May only last a while,

But the taste of your body lingers on…

Like a ship lost at sea frantically searches

For the guiding lights of a lighthouse,

I crave for you when you're not around.

Take me along with you,

Let's explore the mysterious depths together,

And ride the clouds that are heavy with rain.

Let's explore the unchartered tides,

Through fog and storm, and find our shore.

RAPTUROUS DAWN

From the wooden patio,

I gaze at the lavender sky and the milky sea,

And feel the cool ocean breeze kissing my body,

Giving me a million goosebumps.

The Nomade Chloe lingers on,

Leaving a faint aroma of the ecstatic moments

We spent between the sheets.

The Polaris, fixated, looks at us

And commands the clouds to move away

So it can enjoy its voyeuristic morsels

And satiate its carnal instincts.

The lavender sky matches

The color on my neck,

Made by your ravenous nibbling.

The milky sea dances like the way our bodies swayed.

I feel your warm breath on my bare back,

As you pull me back in,

Giving me a million goosebumps.

UNBRIDLED

Unbraid my hair, let the jasmine scent linger on.

Unclasp the pearl necklace, let your fingers run through my neck.

Untangle the knots in my silky kaftan, let my skin breathe you in.

Unfurl the muslin curtains, let the stars envy our secret.

Unravel the mysterious paths that lie hidden,

Let me guide you to the deepest trench.

Unleash the raging deluge, let it overflow.

Unabashed, let us intoxicate ourselves with each other's nectar.

Unquenchable it is, the abysmal depths of desire.

Unbridled...

SILK AND SHADOWS

The night is warm and velvety,

A tender touch on my soft body

Sets the right mood.

Your fingers play the symphony

Of a lover's passionate desire.

My hips sway madly to each note,

Lost in the music of your touch.

Silky shadows shine on the wall,

Illuminated by the glow of the bedside lamp.

Whispers, sighs, moans—

Our mushy bodies melt in sync

With each intimate caress and kiss.

Our fingers intertwine,

Lost in the delicate curves.

The fury of passion rocks us wild,

And then, like shipwreck survivors,

We lie on each other, wet, soaked, spent, alive.

WILDFIRE

It starts with a spark; a raw fire burns slowly,

And before you know it, it intensifies into an untamed wildfire!

Uncontrolled, unpredictable, and unstoppable,

Swiftly spreading, devouring everything in its path.

The forest burns.

Fading echoes whisper through the charcoal-laden trees,

Flames dance in a frenzied, fiery trance,

Passionately engaged in a disastrous union of embers and smoke.

The savage hunger of the blazing fire is finally satiated

By the torrential storm that calms it down, until a spark rekindles.

Desires are like wildfires.

They ignite the restrained instincts of the heart, burning fervently.

Passion consumes us in a conflagration of desires unnamed,

Our bodies wrapped up in this inferno,

With sweltering sighs and reverberating moans,

Till you rain down on me and douse the fire.

Yet, in the wilderness of amorous longing,

Lust-laden eyes crave every inch of you.

Smoldering embers of the tales you narrated

On my bare body with your tongue still linger on,

Until a spark rekindles.

3. CONFUSED

Love is but a mysterious feeling. We tend to idealize our partners and feel ours is a perfect story, we constantly make adjustments, which leads to emotional dependancy.

When the initial madness starts to wear off, and we find ourselves in a situation where we don't really know if the other person values the relationship as much as we do, it can create a lot of confusion. Mixed signals can cloud our judgement, and we often find ourselves questioning everything.

The poems in this chapter bring out the emotional turmoil that one faces when they find themselves in an unstable, insecure relationship.

UNFINISHED

An unfinished poem I crave to complete.

Boulders of memories block my thoughts

Like landslides block roads to a beautiful destination.

I decide to take a detour and start all over,

But the unfinished poem pours gently on me,

Like the soft summer rains.

Petrichor! the fresh earthy scent,

Rainbow! the hues of the heavens,

Soaked in thoughts, I am lost again...

A soft sunshine caresses my heart,

But shadows of doubt leave me in the dark.

A glimmer of hope I find again,

When you promise me

Or love's not a game.

The unfinished verses,

I let them be,

A reminder that sometimes,

You need to trust the uncertainty.

MONOCHROME DREAMS

Monochrome dreams float on the subconscious mind,

Interrupted by randomly scattered pastel shades.

My REM is clouded by vivid images,

I try to paint them on my mind's canvas before I lose them forever,

But everything seems like a messy palette.

All I recall are the monochromes and pastels—

A painter's block...

OBSESSION

For she was his obsession,

The one he vowed to possess.

He brought down the heavens,

Ripped open the heart of the oceans,

And was determined to ignite the flames of love.

He was by her side,

Each morning and every night.

Her vulnerable heart was not allowed to dream,

Of flying away across the stream.

She tried to break free, to soar to distant shores,

And do what she pleased,

But he wrapped the strings around her ribs

And watched her bleed.

He bandaged her wounds, he prayed she would heal,

Yet all he longed to know was her Achilles' heel.

And then he struck, just enough to make her limp,

So he would be the crutch on whom she would lean.

And no matter how hard she tried to get back on her feet,

He knew where to strike so she'd face defeat.

This went on for years, and still goes on,

Somewhere a bird sings a melancholy song.

THERE WAS SOMETHING...

There was something for sure—

Something inexplicable, something overpowering,

Something beyond reason, something we both felt,

Yet instantly tucked away.

Let's keep it that way,

For we both know it's not meant to be.

Maybe another time, in another lifetime, if there is one,

We can be together.

But for now, let's not complicate things;

Let's keep the ending a never-ending story,

For they say,

Unfulfilled love is the purest.

I'M JUST IN LOVE

I wonder why people are afraid of being loved.

Why do they run away when someone showers them with affection?

Is it because they doubt their intentions?

Do they judge them for their actions?

Or is it that they fear if they let them get too close,

They might start feeling the same way?

Can they not understand that love can exist

Without asking for anything in return?

So, if you ever come across someone

Who loves you unconditionally,

Please don't push them away.

It's rare to find someone whose happiness

Is not based on what you give them

But what they can do to see you happy.

They are like the tree that breaks its own branches

So that you can light a fire and stay warm,

Like a rivulet that flows through rocky paths

So you can quench your thirst,

Like a frosty dew drop that stays cold all night

But melts away with your slightest touch.

These might sound like exaggerated ramblings

Of a silly heart to you—

So be it.

You can decide and live with your interpretation.

Meanwhile, I will light another vanilla-scented candle,

Kiss your photo, and dream of us lying down

On pink sands on the islands of Venus.

FOREST OF BLUE

I am lost in a forest of blue,

Not sure which one I love the most.

Maybe it's turquoise,

Like the one the ocean wore

On a wintry January morning,

When we went kayaking?

Or is it cerulean,

Like the one the sky donned

On a sultry May afternoon,

While we idled away our time

Under the old tamarind tree?

Perhaps it's sapphire,

Like the gemstone you found on the sidewalk

On a late September evening;

And we dug up the ground, hid it like a treasure,

Vowing to come back in ten years

To see if it's still there...

But I guess the one I love the most is indigo,

Like the solitary December nights,

Frigid and freezing, just like your heart—

The one I wish I could warm again

With the lambent flames of my love.

I rummage for comfort in the faint, fading hues,

And yet again, I am lost in a forest of blue...

PLACID RESTLESSNESS

Does love make you stronger? I wonder...

Coz no matter how strong I am,

I buckle every time I see you.

I dare not speak of the fantasies I weave...

I try to tame my impish heart

And claw at the ferocity of fate

That brought our paths together,

How I wish we had remained strangers!

My only solace comes from knowing

That you know nothing of my despair,

But if you knew, would you care? I wonder...

I gulp down your thoughts — the ones I recreate each day.

Like paracetamol, they act as a painkiller

And soothe my aching heart.

I pen down my thoughts,

But my whispering wishes,

Choked by yearning,

Impede my train of thoughts,

And all I have are frozen lines…

I am falling short of metaphors,

And like sonatas with no words,

I stop my pen from creating

A fistful of hollow hope.

Will this timelessness of eternal moments,

Where I find us in between the lines,

Ever come alive?

I wonder…

DAUNTING SHADOWS

All you see is a picture with a smiling face,

Do you know, darling, puppets smile too?

But don't be fooled by their pretty smiles—

They have strings attached that make them do what they do.

All you hear is a person singing songs,

Do you know, darling, birds in a cage sing too?

But don't be fooled by their melodies;

Caged birds don't sing odes,

Only lamentations to narrate their miseries.

All you know is nothing at all about how I feel.

I dissolve your thoughts in my restless heart,

Till it flows like blood in my veins;

That's the only way I can feel you closest to me.

I'm afraid if you ever knew about my feelings,

Would you run away from me?

Turn your back on me? Judge me?

Maybe that's exactly what you would do,

And so, I am torn between the two: to confess or to let go?

To return to my old life behind the veil of happiness I always wore,

Hiding scars, bruises, and wounds that have gone sore?

Or should I dive deeper into this surreptitious ocean of love,

The one where you guide me with your smile and gaze,

The one where I want to hold you forever in a loving embrace?

I have no answers; I need none.

All I want to do is breathe and not be judged,

Because remember,

Behind every closed door are a million stories untold...

4. DESPAIR

Love is a powerful mechanism that can throw a person from the highs of the skies to the depths of despair. Being ignored, taken for granted or feeling manipulated can cause extreme emotional exhaustion, emptiness and ultimately a loss of hope.

Fear of losing your loved one, of watching the castle of dreams you built together crumble before your eyes can cause deep emotional stress, and the social obligation of making the relationship seem normal is all the more depressing.

The poems in this chapter bring out the unfiltered and raw pain that cuts through the soul, irregular rhymes scream out the havoc in the mind, and mirror the chaos one experiences when going through this phase.

IT'S THE NIGHT WHEN WE UNITE

It's that night again,

A night when we unite.

I feel the warmth, the wetness,

And the saltiness on my lips.

What begins as a trickle,

Slowly overflows with such frenzy,

That it's hard to control until it's all spent,

Leaving me shivering.

I wipe them away with my bare palms.

It's that night again when we unite—

My tears and me.

SCAM

We are together;

As together as the north and the south poles are from each other.

The four-letter word called love has lost its essence,

It's just a chemical reaction, a hormonal rush—

Nothing but a scam.

No, you don't fall in love; you fall into a scam,

A scam that shows you promises of bright tomorrows,

Makes you dream of rainbow skies,

Wipes away your sorrows,

Lures you into happily ever afters.

But once you've fallen prey to the scam,

It will start revealing its true colors.

The rainbows will turn colorless,

The void of trust will be deep and inky black,

Dreams will crumble before your eyes.

Your heart encased in coal, promises turned to ash,

Like castles in ruins, you will lose your identity,

Your self-respect, your sanity.

People will mock you,

Because you knowingly walked into this scam,

Singing melodies that love is blind.

Now those songs have turned into dirges,

And you realize you are just a pawn

In this scam called love...

PURPLE MEMORIES

She was in love with everything purple,

From flowers to wall colors,

From clothes to shoes.

To her, it was the most intriguing hue,

Made of black, pink, red, and blue.

She knew all along that purple was her color,

The color of joy, peace, love, and valor.

She believed that love blooms best in purple,

And so, she waited for her shining knight.

They met on a purple evening,

A dream had come true,

Everything felt right.

Years have gone by,

The dreams have died.

Yet, purple has stayed as her true companion.

When she lays awake during the long nights,

The dawn breaks with a purple sky.

When the sun sets on the horizon,

It bids her a purple goodbye.

The bruises on her body are a beautiful purple,

The scars on her soul a deeper purple.

She tries to wash them away with her tears,

And slowly they fade, but leave behind

A bit of black, pink, red, and blue...

INTIMATE STRANGERS

They met as two strangers,

They felt the adrenaline rush,

Their eyes held that long lasting gaze,

Their hearts pounding, cheeks blushed.

The journey was but a short one,

From strangers to soulmates,

Promises were made of eternity

And to belong to each other always.

She shared her darkest secrets,

She let the demons out,

She believed that he could slay them,

She believed him without a doubt.

Her belief though was short lived,

As her greatest fears came true,

With open eyes she saw them,

Her nightmares now haunting her blues.

Her secrets were written all over the wall,

She became a laughingstock,

She tried to break down the walls,

But the walls were made of rock.

She bruised herself in anguish,

He laughed, she languished.

He hurled the demons back at her,

One after another,

As strangers they had met,

As strangers they now live,

He with his pride,

She with her grief.

EMPTY UNIVERSE

Decathect: To withdraw one's feeling of attachment as an anticipation of future loss.

Did you know this word existed?

I didn't. I didn't even know such a feeling existed,

And yet here I am, trying to decathect myself from you —

Your eyes, your voice, your presence, your absence,

Your cold responses to my feeble questions,

Your judging mind towards my helpless state,

I didn't see this coming.

Yet I do not blame you,

I never can, never will.

For you do not know the depths of repressed emotions,

The ones that I carefully hid in the attic for over four decades,

The dust had settled on them,

Thick as a quilt woven by experienced hands,

Not wanting to move or see the faintest glow of love's gentle flame.

And no, I won't talk about those anymore,

I never have, I never will...

For fear you might think it's just another excuse

And judge me yet again.

So, I pick up the broken pieces

Of the memories that I gathered of you,

And wrap myself in them.

And I know I would never ever feel your warm embrace,

But neither did I want your cold shoulder.

If only you knew that all I ever want for you,

Is to see you happy with the ones you love

Who make up the universe in which you dwell;

The ones who mean everything to you,

The ones who are the rhythm of your heart.

I kneel in prayer each night and each day,

To ask God to give you everything you desire.

I do not want to be a part of it.

Between choosing what's right and what's desirable,

I'd always choose the first option,

Even if I have to live in an empty universe.

It's painful but that's the only way to keep it chaste.

And the last thing I would want is for you to

Taint my sacred feelings with merciless judgements,

Yet I do not blame you,

I never can, never will...

ALL GOOD

I see grey more often now whenever I look in the mirror.

The sunset years are dawning on me.

These laugh lines are now turning

Into perfectly creased wrinkles.

I see them around my eyes too.

My cheeks no longer have the glow of youth,

My hands are rough and my legs have brown patches.

Yet, the color of my heart is still green;

As green as the meadows we saw in the Valley of Flowers.

The color of my dreams is still blue;

As blue as the poppies we found at Hemkund Sahib.

The color of my hope is still pink;

As pink as the first rose you gave me when I was 16.

And the color of my tears is still red;

As red as a bleeding heart can be.

We shared two decades and a half together,

That's a long-time investment you know?

But maybe it wasn't a wise one,

And hence we are here,

At a crossroad today,

Where one wants a way out,

But the other wants to stay...

Where one has given up,

Yet the other wants to find a way...

Where one can't stand the sight of the other,

And the other one still longs to see their face...

And no, there's no point in making someone stay

Who wants to leave so bad.

I get it!

What I don't get is, why does it have to be this way?

How did we end up like this?

A million questions pop in my head,

I try to fight them all.

I put on a smiling face and face the world each day,

And pretend everything is okay,

And anyone who asks me how I am,

I have a perfectly rehearsed reply, "All good!"

But nothing is ever going to be the same again...

Nothing will feel the same again.

The hurt is real, the pain invisible.

The tears are real, the emptiness invisible.

The darkness is real, a ray of hope invisible...

I look at the mirror which shows a reflection

Of a person I don't recognize,

I see grey and brown and hollow eyes,

But when I face the world outside, to anyone who

Wants to know how things are, my reply will still be

"All Good!"

BETWEEN YESTERDAY AND TOMORROW

These anti-depressants don't work anymore.

I still pop one, and hope I can fall asleep.

Getting tired of finding new hobbies now...

I'm done with painting, candle-making,

Writing, playing the ukelele, learning a new language,

And the other dozen things I must have done

To keep myself busy through the night.

I am done with all of these,

Night after night after night...

Somewhere between yesterday and tomorrow,

I long to find a day where I can be me,

Just me.

I fight hard to not lose the remnants

Of the person I used to be,

But the fabric of wounds is woven with care,

In the lines of my poems, naked truths are laid bare.

YEMBERZAL

What can come from a love that's unrequited?

Harsh winters and frozen tears.

So I buried my feelings deep in the ground,

In the graveyard of my desires.

But Spring came along, singing a familiar song.

What can the Yemberzal's heart do?

All it needs is a bit of sunshine and the fresh morning dew.

The Mazaar-posh bloomed daintily in the graveyard

And opened its pale eyes.

It felt the same rush as I did when I saw you the first time.

Yet, what can come from a love that's not yours?

Bittersweet pain and salty tears.

While the Yemberzal rejoices at the arrival of Spring,

It's the Tulip that adorns the heart of Jannat-e-Jahan.

And so, the unloved Yemberzal,

Bids Spring a farewell.

It's time to let go…

5. HOPE

A famous author once wrote — nature repairs its own ravages. The heart can do so too. After all the emotional roller-coaster, it strengthens one to be resilient in the face of trials, to be determined to find the light in darkness, and to find hope and find yourself again.

This journey is often a new beginning, one that transforms a person, like diamond forged by fire.

The poems in this chapter celebrate the new you, the power of positivity and the healing that comes when one realises life is worth much more than drowning in misery. May you find your healing verse, may you find hope, may you find your Elysian Dream!

LIBERATION

I stare at the place where you stood a while ago,

And rewind our last conversation

I replay it all over in my mind.

What's strange is that even in your absence,

I feel your presence.

Even in your silence,

I hear the unsung melodies.

The letters I wrote with red petals

Enclosed within, are still kept in my diary —

The red one that I carry...

I want to be as away from you as I can,

Coz that's the only way to save myself

From drowning in the abyss of grief.

As forever yours will never be us.

I, the songbird and you, the shrub.

In this game of mindless pursuits,

You forgot a simple truth,

I have wings, you have roots.

BROKEN WINGS

A free bird she was, or so thought she.

Her wings were ready for a flight,

Just as they were meant to be.

But he held her in his firm grip,

And promised he would keep her safe,

She knew deep down something didn't feel right,

She knew he might once again play with her fate.

Alas! She fell for his bait!

He clipped her wings, and made her wait.

He promised to let her soar the skies,

But only when he felt the time was right.

But now no more games will be played.

She is neither weak nor afraid.

You cannot take what belongs to her

No matter how hard you try,

Just so you know,

Broken wings can still fly!

SILVERY REVERIE

I hear the waves crashing on the rocks,

The rhythmic swish of the waves turns into a deep roar

As it pounds against the rocks.

A million broken shells lie scattered on the shore,

Like the pieces of my heart, that I now sit to gather

I taste the saltiness of the silvery waves

That splash upon my face,

But the tears that fall from my eyes taste bitter.

I close my eyes as I trace the silhouette of us,

Enjoying nights like these,

But I quickly open my eyes to life's realities.

I enjoy the freedom of being just by myself

Where I can fly on butterfly wings,

Sing the songs that canaries sing,

And walk barefoot on daisy fields,

And dream of never-ending Springs

The clock strikes 3 and jolts me out of my reverie.

As hardened as it may be,

I still have my heart which beats just for me.

HEALING

Your broken heart pains today

And you wonder if the pain will ever go away.

Your bleeding eyes are drowned with tears

And you wonder if you can ever stop crying.

But please don't give up.

Remember, the rivers dry out too,

So will your tears.

That beautiful phase of your life was not permanent,

Neither is this.

Things will change,

You will heal.

And then you will look back and smile

At how bravely you faced it all and still are...

NATURE'S RETREAT

Amidst the whispering mountain winds,

A soulful symphony of trees begins,

The meadows sway in a peaceful ballet,

The velvet violets bloom in a vibrant vale.

This tangled heart cries in despair

Like a weary wanderer whose soul is impaired.

The heart may be wounded,

But the soul is not weak.

I seek solace in nature's retreat.

I embrace Apricity's allure

And find my elixir,

I find my cure.

Never give up on yourself,

Though life may seem harsh

Remember, it's just another season

This too shall pass....

WILDFLOWERS

The land was but a rocky one,

In stark contrast to the lush valleys

That adorned the Satpura ranges,

Where sheep grazed and maidens played

And painters romanced their canvases.

I hiked along the rocky range.

The trail was hidden, forbidden, forgotten

Accursed it was, or so it felt.

But then I stopped and noticed colours,

Purples, whites, yellows and blues.

Life is a miracle; they proved it true.

The flowers bloomed, despite the rocks,

Devoid of nurture, yet smiling at life.

I learned something from them

That everyone should know,

Always be optimistic all the way through,

If the wildflowers can do it, so can you!

BOHEMIAN SOJOURNS

My bohemian heart wandered through the labyrinth

Of celestial flowers that fell from the heavens.

I admired each flower in awe; it's beauty unrivalled!

The radiant sparkle of the Amethyst clusters,

The strawberry red petals of the Chrysoberyl,

The brilliance of the moonstone blossoms,

And with each step I took, I gathered another flower,

Exquisitely divine and precious like gems.

I placed them gently on the folds of my scarf,

Until I could hold no more.

The 146 moons of Saturn could not match

The dazzling aura I held in my hands.

The orbits in a parallel universe spiralled outwardly,

As if trying to reach out to me and absorb me into their realm.

But I rode on the incandescent clouds

And descended on an Arcadian paradise

Where the flowers crystallized

Into souvenirs of my Bohemian sojourns.

The enchanting dream set me free,

I opened my eyes to a brand new me.

I looked inside my soul and realised,

Every pain in my heart had crystallized.

With the break of dawn, and my curtains drawn,

New beginnings welcomed me.

ELYSIAN DREAMS

My poems no more scream out in pain.

My verses are now infused with fragrant magnolias

That bloom in the sacred garden of timeless memories.

For each day I gather crystalline stars

To create an asterism that illuminates my sapphire nights.

And in the iridescent glow of the pink moon

I hold my diary close to my heart.

The pages are almost over,

Filled with poems of anguish and despair,

But like a fairytale, it will now have a happy ending,

As I weave poetries that need no rhymes,

Only unsaid words that now make their way

On the pages of bright tomorrows.

A flickering desire creeps in softly,

But I sweep it aside, no longer craving

Feelings that are best unknown.

There is no pattern in my poems

And that is liberating,

My Elysian dreams are sprinkled with stardust.

My blues are painted with coral hues,

And with radiant dazzles

I look forward to new tomorrows...

Summary

I hope you enjoyed the emotions expressed in Soulful Serenade, and were able to reflect on your own experiences. I hope you can clear the dust of time and go back to life's profound moments and subtle whispers.

As you close this book, may you carry with you the quiet strength found in these lines, a reminder of the inner resilience and boundless grace that shapes our shared human experience. May these poems serve as a gentle companion, encouraging you to find serenity in your own journey.

Thank you for accompanying me on this voyage.